Rizen Storm

© 2013 by Katrina Morris.   All rights reserved.

Published by Vantage Point Publishing
Indianapolis, IN 46218

No part of this publication may be reproduced or transmitted in any form or by any means, electronic or mechanical, including photocopy, or any information storage and retrieval system, without permission from the publisher. The only exception is a brief quotation in printed reviews.

Limit of Liability/Disclaimer of Warranty: While the publisher and author have used their best efforts in preparing this book, they make no representations or warranties with respect to the accuracy or completeness of the contents of this book and specifically disclaim any implied warranties of merchantability or facilities for a particular purpose. No warranty may be created or extended by any persons. The advice or strategies herein may not be suitable for your situation. You should consult with a professional where appropriate. Neither the publisher nor author should be liable for any loss of profit or any other incidental damages, including but not limited to special, consequential, or other damages.

This is a work of fiction. Names, characters, businesses, places, events and incidents are either the products of the author's imagination or used in a fictitious manner. Any resemblance to actual persons, living or dead, or actual events is purely coincidental.

ISBN 978-0-9883939-6-7

The publisher would appreciate notification where errors occur so that they may be corrected in subsequent printing and/or editions. Please send comments to the publisher by emailing to biz@vppublishing.com

Printed in the United States of America

RIZEN STORM

by Hurricane Katrina

Acknowledgement

To Joshua, Jadah, Danielle and Isaiah, you are the reasons I live, love, and dream. To my grandma Earline Scippio who is gone too soon, rest in paradise. And last but not least, to God be the glory. 1LoVE

Truth without proof

Listen very closely,
these are not just well put together words
to entertain the ear of a listener
This is the depth of my soul that burst to be told,
the moment and opportunity foretold of an ancestor,
The revelation of wisdom entrusted to me
since before eternity was a place of promise
The absolute thoughts and knowing's of truth
but without proof

Who am I?

My name is Katrina
I'm a storm that's rising
that can't be held back
Fuck your walls, barricades and levees
You won't see me coming till I'm right up in your face
and by then it will be too late
I make the whole world pay attention
Take heed to every move I make
I'll have every bone in your body shiver and quake with fear
From the moment you hear that I plan to rearrange some things
I plan to make history
Giving every man his story to tell
While raising hell
You brought it on yourself
Underestimating my potential
Cause I had no credentials
No documents attesting the truth of my wrath
So I let loose of not half
But all that I have
From every wave of the hand
That stretched forth to land
As I stand on waters
Breaching borders
That was meant to keep me out
Now it is your doubt that welcomed me in
And it is its twin dubiety
Being that unsure society
That gave me ground to run through
Now I surround your views and what not's
Because what's not obvious to the eye Is the tears of joy that I cry Flooding your existence
With a force that's persistent I'm one to be reckoned with
I don't play that second place shit
So catch a swift of my ass as I past
To be known as the best or at least one of them

None the less
I don't come to play games
I put out flaming fires that was set to ruin desires
And while you knew not of me
Before I embrace the scene
I was being prepared for such a time as this
Such a time as right now
Forcing you to think how could this nobody you titled
Break free from the bridled restraint
And run her own course
Like a free riding horse
How could that little rain cloud everyone ignored
Have jaws floored cause of the damage and
Belongings that needs be restored
How could that breeze that barely moved leaves
Pick up speed to blow down house and parked cars
Have you looking for your spouses to nurture scars
I would say you were in the wrong place at the wrong time
But it was meant to be Just for you to see me rise from nothing
And I had to compromise nothing
Not my integrity
Didn't have to fuck no celebrity
Refused to change my identity
And collectively
I had to compromise nothing
It was my sacrifice and determination
As I plan to be known to nations
You will remember me
And you will never forget how I made you feel
How I spilled every fiber of my being
Onto the scene
I'm sure you know what I mean when I say
I am here
In body and in spirited
I only want to make a difference
I only want to be heard
And when I speak

I choose my words wisely
That way if they hit you If they miss you
If they effected you
Or protected you
They were meant to do just that for you
I never wanted to shut down and put out some people
That wasn't my intention
But I recall the times I mentioned that I am somebody
And I'm just as important
But you laughed to my face
And even behind my back
So I gave it all I got
Now the end result is
I had to wreak havoc to get you to see me
hear me
Feel me
And understand me
Please don't make it a habit
Of trying to hold me back
It's your force that I challenge
It's that voice that told me to sit stay and die
And never rise from the ashes
That was meant to bury me
From the womb that hoped to miscarry me
But I'm not going nowhere
You will remember me
And every time someone fix their lips to ask who am I
You will tell them
That is Katrina

In between

Yesterday stares at my back side
as I walk away and into what's ahead
Calling me to come back to what was offered
but I ignore its offer instead
Refusing to let it be that rock that close me in
between that hard place
Anticipating that check point to quench what's needed along
this race

Patiently awaiting us

I miss being touched by you,
being held by you,
being kissed by you,
looking into your eyes and becoming one with you,
then he with a capital T.r.u.t.h speaks
and tries to convince me that we have never met
but I'm sure of many different occasions
We have simultaneously breathed the same air,
shared the same space
and exhaled for the same reasons,
Chasing stars is the same thought I fell asleep to,
for the sky is the limit and even in that truth,
he who is shy redefines and pushes the limits
to the heavens and beyond is where he and I respond
to our destiny,
hoping it manifest itself,
putting an end to the prolonged need for he and I to be US,
within him lies all that is needed for I to be inspired and fly
higher heights, but until then I write
with the hopes that the revelation of his essence
comes back to me anchored and revealing
for the whole world to see
because these moments we share can give rise to charity
for a place of locked down love
Chocolate thighs being fondled by masculine hands
on the backside of vivid dreams
seems like out of reach for the ordinary
but his subconscious state of mind accommodates
all which is extra forcing him to be the extraordinary,
every time I visit this place where he patiently waits
for my guaranteed return,
stars shine brighter,
heavenly lights become whiter,
burdens of this world fade into a lighter load,

complete loss of control,
like the raging waves of the storms within my heart's desire,
 or like the fury fire that burns so rapidly
consuming every fiber of my being,
while being right here,
right now in this dream
that is overwhelming at times
because I catch a glimpse of he who chases me
like I'm the brightest star in the sky,
there have been times he has called me Sirius,
or did he say I'm serious,
referring to the breathless moments
he has replied that he wants me,
that request is uttered after he gets the picture
but I ask myself if he really gets the picture I try to paint for him
to let him know that he has me
and I'm not going anywhere,
this dream has now become my reality,
but even in this new found reality
I must sleep
which forces me to be apart from him once again
but I have nothing but no complaints paired with patience,
and as I sleep I'm an artist
who paints a beautiful picture of us in the sky,
it's similar to the night of the 4th of July
so until I find proof to establish facts with Truth,
I will close my eyes and come back to where you lie
waiting patiently for me.

Why are you here?

The first thought through my mind was,
why are you here?
Please don't tell me that
you foolishly mistaken me for a loose woman
or better yet a floozy
Now I'm feeling offended ,
forcing me to get long winded because
you obviously didn't see the line drawn in the sand of new
grounds and unknown territories,
while you're rushing to build houses and park your cars
on land that you never even purchased
land that you've never even thought ahead
to give bread for ownership
but instead, you came with intentions,
to lay foundations,
to listen to the temptations
and have sexual relations,
not knowing that I know you want to be in and out
and on to the next one as if I'm a gas station,
you couldn't even bring roses or carnations to
act as decorations in
this house that you wanna build on
this land that you've never even purchased.
Now I am offended,
you got me standing here looking in your face
as if you're about to say no harm intended,
But maybe it never dawned on you,
the harm it can do
By not carefully treading these grounds
before you begin to drill downtown
And now the more I think about it,
the more I realize you never once cared if these grounds were
safe to walk on,
which leads me to believe you never planned to stay long
So...why are you here

Don't worry
I'll wait
Although what you're about to say Is
far from the truth
That you might have gotten away with
Years ago in my youth
But I know the game
And the same lies told
To lay up in my bed
Just to rest your head upon my bosom
Giving you the best time of your life
For what?
I'm not asking for your money
Not in need of shopping sprees
But give me eternity of love
Is that too much to ask for
For you
It is
It's too heavy
To carry
It takes a real man
To know that
A real woman wants real love
Above all else
So again I ask
You know what
Never mind
I can't spend no more time
Listening to another bold face lie
So I'm just gon say goodbye

My 1st Love

Spending time with my first love
While locked out of heaven
We went rolling in the deep
To find his confession
We stumbled upon diamonds
Shining under full moon
Un identical butterflies
Hatched from one cocoon
Innocent beauty
Like Joan of Arc
Waits in Marvin's room
Turning tables in the dark
But turn on the lights
To search no more
To see the conflicting twins
Named Love and War
Having 2 reasons
To read the writing on the wall
Just the two of us
But ain't no sunshine when I call
Leaving a chain of fools
With grenade in hand
Having to act like a woman
But to think like a man
Pretty blue eyes
Cries save me from myself
My mean green
Contribute to a rising star's wealth
What am I to do
Cause ain't no church in the wild
And where am I to go
And who will save my child
Needing motivation
Its an emergency
I just might wait here

Up under the umbrella tree
But while I wait
I put a spell on you
Now you're drunk on love
Not knowing it's déjà vu
This is just part one
Of me spending time with my man
But know that I was here
Until we meet again...

My Haikus

My country morning
Filled with harmonic nature
Kisses from the sun

My country morning
Visions of the greenery
Blesses the moment

My country morning
Freshest, crisp air I inhale
Unspeakable peace

My country morning
It and I have became one
God has smiled on me

Grind on me

He said
Baby girl
Would you grind on me
Whine for me
 Move those hips
Left to right
Forward then rewind for me
I said
That's what I came here for
I'm all yours
But not unconditionally
Cause there are conditions
Fulfill my premonition of a good time
Hold me by the waist
And forget the time and place
We exist in now
Cause I'm bout to show you how
To die to current affairs
But I must say beware
Of the possibilities
And how I'm capable
To have you in a place you may never want to leave As my back is arched And my ass sway side to side I won't hide the seduction in my every move We will collide with aggression Leaving our bodies bruised

Portrait of me

He asked to paint a portrait of me
I said
Under one condition
See me for who I am
And duplicate the true definition of me
No illusions or trickery to fool the eye
Expose the confusions that try to hide and disguise
In my mind
No white canvas
Just a scarred up black board
That records every imperfection of me
Why not
That's all they choose to see
They're blind to the beauty that's deeper than skin deep
The potential that lies within to reap what it sows
And shows the future to those who cares to see
I would say put the past behind me but
Mankind see my yesterdays
As my right now's
In spite how
My right now's are different from my yesterdays
Paint the blood in my veins crimson red
And instead of a whole heart
Show the hole in my heart that shattered it into pieces
That's left me with pieces of a heart beat
Paint beautiful roses and carnations
To not just be decorations on this battlefield
Between will and won't
Or do and don't
But show the details of each layered petal
And the trebled danger it holds
Because of its vulnerability and fragile state
If it unfolds
Paint my insecurities as low dark clouds in the sky
After all It was the hand of a man that sat them so low

Choked them so slow
To where liquid drops streamed from within and
Screamed for the end of agony and pain
While rain descend onto fertile grounds
Use the most vivid colors of green for my grass
Because this is the other side that's greener
Not because its perfect or better than anyone else's
But it took a whole lot of shit
To be authentic
Creating relentless defenses
Draw a rabbit hole between the two worlds I live in
And the tug of war rope connecting the two
With the cape of good hope in a birds eye view
Cause the mother land is a part of me
Although I watch my back
Cause on the other hand
They throw darts at me
Oh how I love the irony
And last but not least
Display four precious jewels in my right hand
Representing the reasons I stand and faint not
Like the hand of God has ordained that I stand and faint not

Love on display

Oh Father
Temptations never fail to tempt me
Sinful relations prevaileth much of thee
So I stand pleading for your grace and mercy
Not because I deserve it or worthy of it
But because I need it
Like the air I breathe or
Like limited substance to the greed
Chasing after it like a drug
Wanting it
To flow through my veins like the precious blood of
The sacrificial lamb
Who has died for me
Cried for me
Laid down His life to be a guide for me
I've done many things
But never will I take it for granted
Never will I stray from what has been granted
And that is one love, your love
It's the reason I continue when I want to give up
Give up on this world and its reprobate mind
Trying to define my place in it
But since the beginning I've felt misplaced in it
Cause I will never be of this world
And I'm more than just a girl who falls short
More than my troubled past
More than the trials and tribulations that neglect to surpass my purpose
I am blessed beyond measure
Having the pleasure to not be blind to your love on display

Goodbye Love

Every time
I tried to leave
You'd plea with me
For another chance and
Because I love you
I gave you that
Knowing that I was
Just prolonging the end of us
Giving in to your infamous question
Do you love me?
Most things slip my mind but
I remember the exact time I knew
That I was wrong about you
After time has been invested
Future plans has been suggested
But deep down inside lies doubt of happiness
Between you and I
Fate then took over
And brought out the worst in me
Cause I couldn't leave on my own
Untamed anger manifested into this bitch that you grew to hate
Now got you questioning if I'm still your soul mate
Then one day
The ass that I gave you to kiss
Was no longer what you wanted
Then you tapped into your worth
Wanting more than what I had to offer
Much needed birth of a conclusion to us
Hope had changed into an illusion for us
So now this time
You left
Turning tables
With the shoe on the other foot
Force feeding me a silent goodbye
And although I cry

Missing our dysfunctional love
I know it's better this way
And I didn't just learn that...
I knew that for a long time now
I just couldn't see how
To walk away like you did
But I'm glad you could for the both of us But I must say goodbye Love

Mixed feelings

Leaving my mind unstable
Labeling my present moment
As nowhere or now here
I don't know the difference
The disappearance of love have me in a trance
I'm starting to believe love never had a chance
To get to know me
And even when I tried to show he who claimed to love me
He was always too blind to see me
For who I am
And every time I was who I am
and not who he thought me to be
I fell short of being perfect for him
Leaving my heart without a purpose
Certain that without love I'm nothing
Loving the irony of it
The pain in its absence Is paired with unbalance thinking
Drinking away sorrows
Wanting to give up on all tomorrows
Day dreaming
Transforming into incubus horror
I blame no one but self
Health and wealth is what I should've asked for because
Expecting someone to love me
When I love me too much to change for anyone
Is the truth of the matter

Star lights fade

Maybe not in this lifetime
Or in the famous nursery rhyme
But star lights fade
As beautiful as they appear
With forever promises
And anonymous intentions
What's the distance between you and it
Is the question
Never fool yourself, thinking you can catch it
Too quick for the eye
And if you ever catch a glimpse of it
Know that it's just a glimpse
Incomplete view
Or vague indication
Out of the blue
Meaningless flirtation
Cease to fall for it
Cause it won't fall for you
Shooting stars are not shooting stars
Just a misconstrued point of view

I ask myself

What keeps me here?
The battle is so damn brutal
Crucial conflict within
At wits end
I stand
On this end
Of fading lines
That defines nothing
No concrete meaning
Of what this present moment is
Tears drip from face
Like rain of the eavesdrop
As fear eavesdrop on this present moment
I ask myself
What is it about the now
That's too heavy to bare
Downward spiral
Decline is now here
Or is it nowhere
Kindled flame
That burns from the inside out
Manifesting into doubt
So I ask myself
Why do I ask myself
When I already have the answer

Untitled
Breaking the heart of a girl
Is like clipping the wings of angel
Leaving her with the task
To find another way to not stay down

I was just a girl

I was just a girl
Who knew no better
And no better knew me
Like a permanent mark
On the back side of its hand
I was just a girl...
Violated in ways
At the time I couldn't understand
Holding on to my confusion
Of what love is
While never letting go of bottled up tears
By the grace of God I was tough
Too tough to let this heavy burden
Be the straw that breaks my back
While laying on my back
Violated in ways I couldn't understand
Nobody ever told me
That this was even a possibility
Of what anyone had to go through
You see I was just a girl
Who knew no better
And no better knew me
Like I was the apple
And it was the tree
It's funny how but not funny how one action
Can bring on a multitude of feelings
Rushed with thoughts
And an endless search for healing
Nobody there to protect me
Which caused me to be more angry
Because my guardian was too busy
To see the pain in my eyes
When I didn't speak up to complain of the times
I was robbed of my purity

Producing insecurity
Abusing my immaturity
Nothing authentic
Something like the yellow brick road
That portrays the streets of gold
Or lust and infatuation
That is often mistaken
For love
But I was just a girl
Who is now a woman
A woman that refuses to allow bruises of my past
Be the face of my future
I am more than just that girl
I am strength birthed from weakness
I am uniqueness birthed from unparalleled circumstances
I am advances from doubt
I am the loud shout from silenced tongues
I am the breath of life in lungs from smoked out wind pipes
I am stars and stripes from a lowered flag
I am more than just that girl
More than just a number to add to statistics
I am the opposite of what should've been
Simply because
What should've been
Was the opposite of what could've been
And although that girl exist no more
Because she died
Just so I can live
And be restored
That girl is never forgotten
 And all that she has endured is not in vain
There's not enough time in the day to explain
My gratitude
Because she not only saved my life
She saved my girls
And the girls of many parents
Bringing awareness

To a muted cry for help
So although she
Who is I
Was just a girl
She is one of many heroes
In this world
Never saying woe
to the desired ball of fire
that passionately blaze
within my heart's desire
from the inside out
then the outside in,
rapidly consuming my world
while at the same time making mends
A young girl
who had given up on love
because I was just a girl,
 Foolishly thinking love had given up on me,
but how could that be
with every day that I see
standing posted waiting is opportunity
to grasp love's destiny
Waiting in absolute divine decree,
patiently for me,
paired with eternal devoir
to maintain ecstasy therefore,
entrusting me with your amour
not entitled to uphold this position
but never doubting that I can,
is that why it's I you choose
cause you know I will withstand

Dear Men of God

I take this opportunity to render tribute from deep within
You are set apart cause you have taken part of spiritual circumcision
You remain strong on stable ground in spite the change of seasons
You see no reason to ever depart from God's supreme vision
what is it that makes you distinct from others? Some people will inquire
It's cause you trust and believe in Elohim and not afraid to go through the fire
You put God first in everything you do, knowing He will come through for you
You stand on His word cause in the depths of your heart you have found Him to be true
It is noticed and admired how you love your wife like Christ loves the church
When have found that good thing, it is you who calls off the search
Jehovah Jireh resides in you, He uses you to provide
You live in production and never destruction cause you don't operate from pride
You are that mighty man of valor, from your pores reap tenacity
God has poured into your past your maximum capacity
You remind me of some important men that have come before you
Ask yourself, if you see yourself, as I take time to name a few
Abraham, was a man who traveled with faith
Joseph, helped raise a son he didn't help create
Peter, didn't let his failures take over and define him
Joshua, crossed over and left the wilderness behind him
Jesus, offered himself as the perfect act of love
And so many more men who is worthy to be spoken of
You understand that the effectual fervent prayers of a righteous man availeth much

You enter into His presence with the expectation of His touch
You are a king who keeps stability for whom you are responsible for
Reminds me of my pastor cause for us he will go to war
Real men of God have learned what it is to die to self and human aims
You have found the ministry of Christ to be much more vital than any ball game
Men mighty in the scriptures lives are dominated by a sense of greatness and majesty
Blessed is the man who trust in the Lord for by the river he is planted like a tree
He is perfect even in his imperfection because he walk not after the flesh
From his heart flows fresh oil cause he has been to the olive press
Let this be nothing more than a recognition that is well over due
Sincerely,
Men of God, I salute you.

Christmas

Christmas, what exactly is it, what does it seems?
Is it the time of the year to find the best sales for a plasma widescreen?
Is it where the snow falls on some parts of the earth for a more magical theme?
Is it where gift giving is the extreme, if you know what I mean?
Some celebrate but delete Christ and calls it X-mas
For some it's the worst part of the year, can you believe it, Christmas?
A surprisingly great number of people become suicidal then back to the dust
The unbearable pressure the world has created has created a royal flush
We put Merry in front of it and forget to be just that
Don't let your gift be what you didn't want cause then you'll turn into brats
Yeah I said, some of you turn into brats It's the truth anyhow and I won't take it back
If asked what is Christmas, very few will say labor
First and far most it is the birthing of our Lord and Savior
although it's the perfect bribe to the kids for good behavior
It is the manifestation of the absolute and impeccable life saver
Christmas is love, for God so loved the world that He gave His only begotten son
Christmas is kindred relationships; family is who there the most just because they're your loved one
Christmas is joy; its great bliss can never be surpassed or outdone
Christmas is travailing; it is where nativity rapidly flows from
All odds were against Mary but she still delivered what was ordained
Not letting her lack weigh her down like a simple ball and chain
The blessed event on that cold night is not difficult to explain

Lets never forget its God giving purpose always keep it on the brain
Always dwell upon the pure blessings of the sweet baby Jesus
For even the star shined brighter as if it was covered with angel dust
All those genuine in heart said to see Emmanuel I must
And no they weren't waiting by the chimney for Old Saint Nicholas
They traveled near and far in the freezing winter cold
They brought their best gifts, some silver and some gold
Just to be a blessing to the miracle that has unfold
Jesus, the reason for the season is the truth the word has told

Change is definite

Some people are apprehensive to the idea of change
Sometimes too afraid to let nature rearrange
Some can catch a glimpse of it from a great distance away
While others can't identify it until it's right up in their face
We attempt to regulate it, convinced that we are in control
But its commodity like time, it sets its own goal
Something simple like the seasons that change with no aid
Even something so ripe can end up decayed
I engage how the days will per mutate into night
Even how our leaders are no longer always white
A change so great that forced continents to split
I believe it's just fate so be willing to submit
Babies are born then eventually they're adults
Frozen cube left at room temp, water is the result
Sam Cooke wrote that a change is gonna come
The hope for the truth is where it originated from
God said He will bring His seed from the east and gather them in the west
Him doing a new is what He does best
When its goodness present itself don't turn the other cheek
Wait for the revelation of its purpose because soon it will speak

Be Thankful

A ten car pile-up on the highway
A little kid didn't get to see another day
Breaking news says another little girl is missing
A lonely wife only wants her husband to listen
A mother's body was found, she was raped and killed
A family of five has no clue where they'll get their next meal
Little Catholic boys are molested by their priest
A single father and his daughter live in the winter with no heat
All these things around us and we still find time to complain
Open up your eyes and maybe you'll see that the whole world is pain
Like for example one household is dying of AIDs
Then right next door, the woman of the house is treated like a maid
Always be thankful cause it could be worst
That could be you going to a funeral and you're the one in the hearse

A Message

What has become of you as a people?
You turn your heads to those who beg and fail to aid the cripple
Is it because you excessively desire to feed the individualist called self?
Oh, the shameful things you have done for power, fame and wealth
You love and worship the dollar bill, you even call it almighty
You know the love of it is the root of all evil and for it is why you are striving
You rob the poor, the rich and those in between and even the Divine Being
You still sleep because you are weak, in desperate need of awakening
You fornicate under carnal knowledge not understanding its acronym
You're like a bird full of fear too afraid to ever go out on a limb
Some have faith but with no works, it won't get you very far
The biggest dreams your kids will dream is to one day be a super star
Mothers and fathers abandoned their children if it's only fair
At one point, you taught your kids to exercise the Lord's Prayer
Your backs are turned to those who desperately cry for help
You see no need for charity so it collects dust up on a shelf
Some of you justify pain brought upon those who are innocent
While others are content with giving God a measly fifty percent
You lie, cheat and steal mainly cause everybody else is doing it
You do a favor for others but only if you can benefit
Let's not forget your acceptance of sex with the same
Not understanding that it was the cause of the city being consumed by flame
Turn from your wicked ways cause your soul is in danger
For I am just the vessel appointed to be His messenger

Attention Fathers

Ever wondered what it is that makes you a father?
It most definitely isn't because you had relations with your child's mother
A father quietly withstands the winter chill and bares the summer heat
He proudly labors for hours to make sure his family has food to eat
A father fosters the young and teaches them right from wrong
Not just physically, but mentally, he teaches them how to be strong
He spend time with his son just to show him the ropes
He instructs on how to shave by first applying the shaving soap
While tending to his daughter, he's lenient and gentle
He understands the time shared cause it's a vital fundamental
To his little girl he's an example on what kind of man she should marry
When his children get tired, it's the father who's willing to carry
In the eyes of his kids, he's a hero without a cape
But only cause in the house that he built, it hangs from the window like a drape

Jehovah

Jehovah Nissi-The Lord my banner
First, let me inform you on the biblical story
The alter that was built in remembrance of victory
As Moses stretched forth his hand the Israelites prevailed
When his hand grew heavy, he sat, and then it was his hand someone else had held
This Jehovah blows in the wind symbolizing a conquering flag
Puts regret in the heart of my opponent cause they wish they never had
When my battle is won it is He who is in the mist
While simultaneously, it is He who lives in the bliss
Jehovah Rophi- The Lord who heals
Restores something back to its normal or useful state
Performs surgery without ever needing to sedate
Heals the land that has been polluted by sin
So that land can now be fruitful once again
That spiritual healing that so many are in need of
Just like David cried out to this Jehovah like a mourning dove
Psalm 147:3 says He heals the hearts that are broken
He binds up their wounds like fabric that has been woven
Jehovah Jireh-The Lord who provides
Yielding a ram in the bush in place of ones only son
He wanted the heart of Abraham and not the life of his loved one
This Jehovah sees the need before it is ever needed
Either before, during or after your "lack of" it is He who has interceded
Providing bread to the hungry and water to those who thirst
Even a financial blessing that need not be reimbursed
Take no thought for tomorrow and trust that it is He who will come through
God will provide every one of your needs especially if it is He you are subject to
Jehovah Shalom-The Lord is peace

That mighty man of valor has seen the angel of the Lord face to face
Peace came upon him so he built an alter in that same exact place
In the moment of distress it is He who desires to abide
He's not one of counterfeit, He is and always will be bona fide
Perfect peace penetrate the heart of a man
It surpasses all comprehension this carnal mind may never understand
Granting us Himself in every circumstance
Tranquility and serenity is what He loves to enhance
Jehovah Rohi-The Lord my shepherd
A psalm of David says that I shall not want
Because He is my perfect keeper, I'm free to be nonchalant
It is He who will search for the lost and bring back the strays
Because He is who He is, I will acknowledge Him in all my ways
He guides me to fresh soil to feed and to breed
His rod and His staff comfort me indeed
He makes way for my cup to run over
While at the same time I still remain sober
Jehovah Ezer-The Lord my help
It is He whom which I lean on cause His arm will not be far off
Without Him I can do nothing so I trust Him at all cost
As a branch cannot bring forth fruit except it abide in the vine
No more can I, except I abide in Him, my availing divine
Like David said I shall yet praise Him for the help of His countenance
Now seeing how he could offer up a sacrificial praise of dance
Please know that the Lord is the sustainer of my soul
My rock of refuge when I'm in need it is He who takes control
Jehovah Tzadekenu-The Lord our righteousness
Every good form that makes me who I am
This Jehovah reveals Himself in the sacred precious lamb
The one who is sinless, just and innocent
He carried our sins on the cross which makes Him that perfect represent

It is He who stands before the Father and ask to see us faultless
but only if we operate in He, then shall we be called justice
It's His presence from which all blessings flow
If not accepted into the heart of us, then we may inhabit a dwelling down below

What I seek

Mr. Pilot I have my ticket and I don't care where you go
Just take me far from here where my name, no one knows
Chicago, Paris, London or Japan
I could care less it could even be Afghanistan
The place where I'm at was never intended for me to stay
Trust me when I say that I just want to be on my way
Please don't assume that I'm running from my past
I now know happiness here was never going to last
I denied that truth when it first showed its face
That same truth I stand here ready to embrace
Maybe you can suggest a place that's just right for me
It has to be somewhere I can live for eternity
I'm tired of traveling, moving from here to there
If you won't take me, I'll walk, on the search to find the stair
If they ask you if you've seen me, the truth is what you speak
You tell them that I've left this place because love is what I seek…

Snowman

Only for a season you inhabit my world
Your big, stony eyes portray golden pearls
Your stretched sharp nose I love to kiss
When you come to me it's hard to resist
I have the power to put a smile on your face
You're a work of art belonging in a display case
Thinking you will go nowhere cause you have no legs
But eventually I wake up and somehow you have fled
You've left the things I invested in you where I saw you last
Going from a hope for our future to now an image of my past
Until we meet again is rooted in my heart
Because I understand why you had to depart
Why you will only be my seasonal snowman
Cause you can't take the heat of being my real man

Slave

Chained and silenced
is the truth of my right now
by the one who holds not only the key to my freedom
but the key to my heart
that screams free them,
some ask who is them that my heart speak of,
first and far most
it is love paired with fire and desire
chocked by infatuation that refuses to transpire,
while he refuses to allow me to be free,
I contemplate the day I'm pulled close
by the masculine hands
that holds me bound to the ground
but instead of a detained approach,
he recognizes the admiration in my eyes
if he would just look me in my eyes,
these voluptuous lips anticipate the kiss
from he who seems to be blind
because my love for him is so visible,
but yet I stand here invisible
but seen on a daily bases,
beneath these rags that he clothe me in is a work of art
that patiently wait for the answer to when will my love
remove the chains that make sure I stay and never leave,
every time he comes close
I try to show him that I'm not going anywhere
but every time he comes close
he fails to see that here is where I want to be,
the only place I get to see the man who lives in my dreams,
the one who man handle me till my screams become extreme,
deep penetrations from his release of frustrations
and stimulations from the gentle strangulations,
because that's how I like it,
he gives it to me like he has created it
and I have taken it and rated it

the best I've ever had

Won't find love

Gotcha lips pressed to the rim of that bottle
with your head cocked back,
gathering the essence of the thing you love the most,
you've been trying to catch that wild turkey
not realizing that its caught you,
preparing for the holiday roast,
interacting with the indescribable pain and pleasure
purchased off the top shelf
as if that moment you've exchanged vows
with the irresistible bride who is top shelf quality,
confusing quality with quantity,
consuming the maximum amount of your bride Dahlila
predestined to be your weakness,
predestined to be the wolf in sheep's clothing,
pulling the wool over your eyes
to hide the ticking time bomb,
causing you to love that which hates you
and hates what love you,
allowing it to determine your daily limit,
putting your mind, body and soul in it,
but I can guarantee,
that's the one place you won't find love

Amen Corner

It's impossible to agree all the time
Your opinion is defined
by the beliefs entwined
in the capacity of their mind
Every word they utter is your bread and butter,
feeding off of it like a cub suckling its mother
Where is a mind of your own?
Have your fear for them postponed your idea?
Why do you allow your voice to be overthrown by their tone?
Bowing down,
with their words clutched tight
in the palm of your hands,
fear of letting go cause
maybe then you'd have to stand in solitude
cause no one understand a genius dude
Your point of view is just as potent
but you continue roping a tight knot
around the collar of you as the individualist
trying to dismiss the animate object
that has something to say
opposite what's said
You're better off dead cause you're brain dead,
don't remain fed by the vain
but instead
Get out of the amen corner,
it's not for you.
It's for the weak-minded, yellow bellies, wishy washy crew
That corner is their punishment,
cause they're afraid of an argument,
being the unfortunate subordinate,
making their submission permanent
Get out of the amen corner,
let me be the first to say
that I value your opinion
and at one point you did too.

This is a brand new start to a brand new you
This you will share your wisdom,
not letting it be in vain
You will kill the system that has your voice retained
cause I know you have something more
than a simple yes, ok and an amen

Admiration of a Rose

Bold and divine rooted in the ground
Profound silence resounding a sound
Scales of virtue arranged surround
Crowned poise eternally hound
Individually held in high regards
Adds delicacy to any nurtured yard
Pure enough to lie face a greeting card
White picket fence acts as its bodyguard
Stable axis holds the jewel
Light of the day and water is its fuel
Creates an oasis out by the pool
Foster care is the major tool
Its sweet aroma fills the room
Fills the room of a bride and groom
Imitated in oils and perfumes
The perfect gift is what to assume
Greatly welcomed on any first date
Post winter blooms is what it creates
Beautiful symbol of the New York State
Bought with a price at any given rate
Towards the sky is the way it grows
Not meant to be kept enclosed
Cherished with eyes and nose
My simple admiration of a rose

80's Baby

Momma dancing to The Temptations, Treat Her Like A Lady on the radio.
Your head started to go with the flow listening to Word Up by Cameo
Mrs. Jackson was feeling nasty while her brother was on his Thriller
Boom box was blasting while jamming to Salt & Pepper
Popping the cassette in was nothing foreign then
Now it just seems like way back when
If the colors of your clothes weren't bright and loud
Then you dampened the mood looking like a rain cloud
House Party, Ghostbusters, The Goonies, to name a few
And let's not forget the ole creepy Beetlejuice
The big poufy hair went well with the short poufy skirt
Who didn't want to go to the purple rain concert?
Adjust the antennae for a clear view of The Cosby's show
Rubik's cube would cause fun induced headaches to grow
Carter, Reagan and Bush was in charge of the States
Oprah's rise to her current status could no longer wait
Bill Gates became the first billionaire of micro computing
Memories of those times are what I'm uprooting

Damaged Goods

Where do I begin to express
abused, defiled, corrupt scorching's
of the way my mind perceive life as of today?
I wasn't always this way...
I freely gave certainty to all,
believing that all had my best interest at hand,
high hopes and regards for family, friends and strangers,
foolishly thinking if I'm good to them then I would receive good.
But is that always true?
A lot of the times I gave smiles but got frowns in return.
I gave money but got debt.
 Gave love but got hate.
There use to be a day where you plant apple seeds and got apples.
Is there something wrong with the sower?
I don't think so...
I think it's the corrupt ground,
the deprived lawn
that waits to suck the life out of any source of supplier
that it comes in contact with.
Makes you don't want to put in the labor to sow seed

His name is Music

I make love to him
with expectations of something awesome in return,
burning deep down inside
is a hunger to learn more of him,
paired with elevations
through penetrations of the sounds of this love...
his name is Music.

Woman

Woman
What is it that comes to mind when you think of such a word?
Maybe it's just a voice that is obviously unheard
Maybe a tongue that is silenced in the presence of the masculine
Maybe a purpose that only dwells in the depths of her abdomen
Woman
One that is belittled although she is the carrier of life
She's easily sold to fulfill a need at any given price
She's disrespected everyday as if it's been rehearsed
But let this shine light upon truth to show you just your worth
Woman
My comprehension of you percolates pass the superficial
The realness of you is not defined by your hair that may be artificial
But it is your tangible existence in congeniality
The importance of your existence is more than your fertility
Woman
You are just as relevant as the one who was formed first
Although some only remember that it was you who was coerced
But nevertheless you are the gift that keeps on giving
You are the womb that beauties of life would gladly choose to live in
Woman
I'm reminded of Sarah who bore no child until her later years
When it was all said and done she travailed laughter instead of tears
The Virgin Mary was found blessed and highly favored
She was chosen to birth Jesus Christ my Lord and Savior
Woman
Deborah and Jael was used to help defeat the enemy
Notice that these women bestowal was more than just their beauty
Harriet Jacobs was an escaped slave who later became an author

Harriet Tubman was the Underground Railroad conductor
Woman
What's expected of you is everything less than man
Sometimes you have to prove that you're equal and sometimes better than
Not to bring comparison between us and our opposite
But to our Father we find it easier to be willing to submit
Woman
Woe unto man who would subdue your advantage
You're a force to be reckoned with and not one easily damaged
You have your alabaster box filled with costly fragrant oil
God's favor rest upon you and that is why you're spoiled
Woman

Strength in Numbers

It doesn't take a mastermind to become aware of definite strength in numbers
An organization of a determined population can bring change to reputation minus spoken slander
You can look back in history and see how achievement in unity has made an essential affect
It has gained resources, rights that were denied and most definitely respect, need I not neglect
Dr. Martin Luther King peacefully assembled the oppressed to stand up against the oppressor
W.E.B. Dubois founded the NAACP to profit advancement from the aggressor
Cesar Chavez an icon for the Latino community compelled the movement and protest for workers
Bold women across America strengthened together to become parallel privilege searchers
Must I remind you of the old saying; it takes a village to raise a child
But that belief is no longer so now your daughters are on girls gone wild
Even the miraculous human body enforces and executes on one accord
Many parts and systems but one unit is what we should be moving toward
Never have I seen the hand destroy the ear because of its lack of similarities
They are a union arising from common interest coated with collective solidarities
Being too stubborn or too prideful to come together reminds me of oil and water
Its precise chemistry relentlessly creates an estranged border
Today I address the border that runs rapidly through the color violet
To the left is blue and on the right is red but to come together happens with violence

Lives are wasted on the street or in prisons or six feet beneath the ground
Even the innocent suffer leaving a potential future unsound
To some, the hood you're from wasn't your elected neck of the woods
You landed there by family or friend and stood and said I would
I would be devoted and loyal to a brotherhood of bloodshed
I would be the willing hand to add numbers to the dead
If approached with disrespect I would be the first to pop a cap
I would put my faith in a piece of steel that's why I always remain strapped
It's not unnoticed that you possess consistent dedication and entrepreneurship
Character like that can build a successful and wealthy relationship
Let's eradicate the mentality of dividing what's meant to be whole
Let's commonly strive to one day walk the heavenly streets of gold
Let's give permission to peace love and harmony to freely operate in our lives
You being the supporter of it can be the seed planted nationwide

Hurt

I hurt like a tortured victim
The pain is causing me to weep
Uncontrollably I cry loud
and spare not my pride
Reaching the point of being the broken camel's back
My foe is smaller than the straw,
lighter than the straw and
At this very moment it weighs me down
Am I weaker than it?
No I'm vulnerable and naked
Sometimes I think that is why I weep
Already on the verge of sob
Before the foray
Like a liquid filled balloon ready to burst
But not
Still holding it together
Until an unintended meltdown
Not an expected and watched for needle
But a flame, kindled beneath me
Then before you know it,
I pop I gush forward, I erupt, I disintegrate,
rupturing into pieces
Like the hands of God had written that for me
Nothing I could've done to prevent my tears from falling
I weep like the pain is unbearable
because it is
I hurt like a tortured victim

Last time was the last time

Can't go back to misery
I just want to be free
From the disappointments
Living in suspense
Of lies and deceit
When all you do is cheat
Last time was the last time
Nothing you can say
To make me want to play
This love game with you
I'm ending the dejavu
Repetition of the same pain
Created a permanent crimson stain
On the cloth of my love
But now's the time to get rid of
You in my life
Cause you're nothing but strife
Last time was the last time
No more taking you back
My bags are packed
When I walk out this door
I won't return no more
Last time was the last time

Why?

Sometimes I search for the answer to the question that's inside
Why?
Why am I even here?
Feeling out of place in a world that feeds off my tears
Thriving from the output of energy that escapes my pain
My heart is Able
But the world is Cain

When you're done praying

Prayer
It's the solution to every problem
Needing no substitution
Because it works
Bended knees and bowed head
In the presence of God
With hopes to be led
To blessings of all kind
When body is in need of healing
Or feeling the pressure of situations
Broken hearted from disappointing relations
Or being accused of false accusations
Repeating cycles of cursed generations
Or even needing strength to help fight temptations
Prayer works
Taking your trials and tribulations to the Father
Because He knows all And He can dispose all of your problems
But in between prayer
Is sometimes where the mistake is made
So many things invade your mind
Taking you out of what's divine
Causing you to co sign doubt, fear and complaint
But be reminded of the chosen in the wilderness
Doubting God caused some to miss
The promises that were promised
If you believe in your heart then ignore the eyes
Because sometimes your prize is in disguise
To whom much is given
Much is required
Don't grow tired in your journey to go higher
Keep faith close
Make it a necessity like the oxygen in the air
Being without it would cause you to perish
So use it in your prayer
Never doubt God

I am mother

Nurturing womb that hauled offspring's of my existence
Raising kings and queens
With bare minimum assistance...I am mother
She who with one life to live
But having four lives to give all that I have to offer
That well that dare not run dry
That sail that's strong enough to guide
Along life's sporadic journey...I am mother
That strong foundation
To hold walls and coverings
That shelter from what the outside brings...I am mother
Irreconcilable force of nature
Towards violent behavior
Or any intent of hurt harm or danger...I am mother
The only one that cooks but last to eat
Things that I need take back seat
Teacher of good morals
Peace seeker between childish quarrels...I am mother
Aching pain that forms in the frontal lobe of my brain
When reaching pass the point that maintain peace...I am mother
Living witness of pure genuine love
Blessed with angels from up above
Striving example
That fire of a burning candle
To shine light upon darkness...I am mother
Their guardian
Provider
Over seer
And fighter for all that's right in their life
Delighted by precious laughter's
Watching them chase after fun filled times
Enjoying the bliss in their hearts that spill out onto their face
 As smiles create unforgettable moments...I am mother
Collector of sentimental values

Protector against bumps and bruise
That soft voice they trust
Strong voice fair and just
Random opportunities to disgust
Any and everything because its a must...I am mother
Tough skin that holds in precious treasure
Having the pleasure to fall in love everyday
Since the moment...
I became mother

Inspired by you

You see
There's some things I must get off my chest
Some people have the audacity
To confess with their mouths
And believe in their hearts
That every word they utter
Should not be addressed I beg to differ
Especially those words that
Cut like a double edged sword
Or sting like the bite of a viper
While being left trying to decipher
What part hurt the worst?
Should I be offended that your words
Let me know how you really feel
Or should I keep it real
And let it be known that
Your words are like sticks and stone
That break my bones
Reaching beyond the point of no return
They burn like eternal fire from the pits of hell
Or being that sound you can never get back after you've rung that bell
What I say to you is...
Watch your mouth
And the best way to do that is to be the man in the mirror
You're too busy trying to get a clearer view of my flaws and all
But I can't recall a time when your opinion of me defined
The person I am
Telling me what I'm not and what I can't do
Then turn around and tell me
That I've misconstrued what you've said
Do you feel the need to tear me down?
With adjectives verbs and nouns
Utilizing your freedom of speech
When the point of what you're saying is so far reached

Maybe there's something in me that intimidate you
And that which you see you try to undo
But you can't
Because I am that tree that's planted by the water
Bearing good fruit for sons and daughters
Forever green leaves
Enjoying the breeze
From my sower who has planted seeds of me
What's wrong with nurturing my grounds with hopes that I grow into a better me?
Building me up with at least a mustard seed of positivity
That's what I would do for you
Do you think that judgmental thoughts don't creep into my mind?
To try to define who you are
Think again
The only difference is I have a filter from my brain to my lips that strips down every word that could tear you down
Because truth be told
The same way you integrate your thoughts and your words to form an insult
I've held back my response to your ignorance on impulse
Due to the fact that I'm the better person
Yeah you talk a good game and it all sounds good
But you aught to be a shame claiming that you're misunderstood....

Compared to who?

Standing in contentment due to satisfaction of who I am
This mirror speaks to me says damn
You're a grand slam
Passing it with flying colors as if it was an exam
Ready to take charge like a head butting ram
Need I mind you that is just the tip of the iceberg
I stand here in my own world no with no judgment to be heard
I can stand here all day because my opinion is what's preferred
But I must go out to face the world and try to ignore the word
The word is
To be beautiful facial features must line up in perfect symmetry
To create and manifest
Then assure the beholder perceives harmonies of a heaven-like display
Hour glass frame being 36, 24, 36 holds validation of being erotically attractive and being the only reason asked on a date
The word is...
whatever color skin I'm in perfect range meets in the middle
Too dark or too light grants me a possibly dismissal of a smile
Yes, the smile,
A delighted expression
that is sometimes hid or prevented because of insecurities that has persecuted reasons to contract roughly
17 facial muscles that simply desire to reveal a pleasant thought or moment
An urge to remain in constant combat with everyone
and even myself because the word is
Everyone and even myself is the anti-me opponent
Let's not forget the word that unjustly makes proclamation that the force that gravitation exerts upon my body should be minimized
To not only captivate the attention of the opposite gender but
To intrigue and possess respect and finesse like a hunting lioness in a foxy red dress
Don't get me started on the price you think I'm worth

cause you've calculated the cost of my clothes shoes and purse
Put down the device that you use to tally up the price
Refuse to coerced and forget what's been rehearsed
Who is this ideal personage that I fail to measure up to?
Arrange a time and place to come face to face so that I can see what look to pursue
How should I wear my hair?
What clothes should I wear?
Should I never curse or swear?
Who should I date, baseball, football or basketball player?
Should I be the cool kid who rocks the best gear or
Dare to be the keen and cleaver square?
Oh no I got it,
I should be a combination of them all,
I should be the harlot, who knows Jack, Jill and Paul,
Maybe I'll be short and cute while at the same time I stand tall
and that leading star on stage waiting for her curtain call
No, I got it an apocalyptic epiphany just fell upon me.
Compare me to me
The way that I walk and how the ground responds to every step that I take
Not miscarrying the variations of my weight
My method and course of action that I outline
Refusing to be the lab rat in a maze of avenue that has been defined by you and not I
Compare me to me
Stand under,
I mean understand that I can only be me
Some may question who is this me that I would rather be,
If you think you're ready let me settle the scrutiny because
It is only I who can rightfully decree
That the one and only me is…
Significantly vital
Kinda like a delicate spongy brain
that worry not of invasion because of its firm solid barrier
that crown every necessary febrile unit,
and in spite of how

fragile it really is,
it really is irreplaceable
I'm patient as a flower waiting for the sun to rise
Calm as the day Jesus was baptized
Inflexible as an immoveable rigid rock
Tenacious when it comes to harboring my flock
There is none other
None other Katrina spewed from the shaft of good victory
into the lacuna of a spear ruler
then birthed out of wedlock to witness a clear union
between my creator,
I like me
Although I have flaws and makes mistakes
With downfalls, hurts and aches
I am perfectly me
Every day that I see, that I am still me
Something down on the inside never seize to be pleased
Pay attention and don't let this be
The time that I have told you about me
And you ignore my words to the third degree
While I willingly offer you the master key to me.

"Thirstiness"

Even in the mist of "Thirstiness" and
Disrespect that's been dismissed
It is I who can rightfully say that...
I am yours
Three words that stand true with
No room to misconstrue
My sweet kisses paired with "I love you's"
You are my world within this world
Carrying you on my shoulder
Keeping you closer
Cause that's where you want to be
Need to be
The king in you
Loves the queen in me
And that's no doubt
Just a guarantee...

Spell on me

You put a spell on me
I can never leave
No matter what you put me through
You cheat
You lie
Love when I cry
Then tell me its gon be alright
You put a spell on me
Potions that
Control emotions
Buried deep down in my soul
Leaving me to be
Like a puppet
Your hand up my back like
I'm a Muppet
Or like a rag doll
That's constantly poked with
Joked with
Roped high
To hang low
Gathered round to watch me die slow
I swear when I'm not looking you're
In the kitchen cooking up a brew
Tasty concoction
Mistaking it for stew
Having rituals over my name
Practicing voodoo
Mind control
Every single time I wanna leave
I feel your strong hold
I'm the victim of imprisonment
Feeling like I have no legs
To walk out the door that's
Obviously open but instead
I stay

Cause I feel like I can't leave
I look around to break free
From the chains that
Must have me bound
But there's no chain to be found
It's like I sold my soul
And I no longer belong to myself
Forfeiting my present help
Not knowing if I'm coming or going cause
All I think about is you
Every blink of the eye
Beat of my heart
Breathe in my lungs it all belong to you
Leaving me with one option
That is if I leave
I just might die
So I stand here with
Deep sighs and
Teary eyes
Because being here is just as painful
Mistreated
Defeated by your
Starry eyes and
Pretend cries
And even when I have reason
To walk out the door
And never look back
I look back before I reached the door
Being that pillar of salt but I swear its not my fault
The spell I'm under is heavy
And the place I'm in is dry
Like walking through the dessert with an elephant on my back
Chasing after he who leads me
To a world of pitch black
I know you have a spell on me
When I'm asleep I hear you chanting
It makes me weak

To you demanding
Me to stay and never leave
But one day
I promise
I will break free

Music

Watching a live band,
I began to catch myself fall in love with that man
who gently holds the neck of his bass guitar,
stroking up and down while he plucks and tugs on the strings of my heart.
I ask myself if he knows the feeling I feel.
Wanting to hold on to the rhythm he creates,
while not needing a mad vocalist to translate,
exactly what he's saying,
cause rather than hearing the lyrics to understand this man,
I feel the beat through my veins
replacing the heart beat
I can't explain the fact that,
for this very moment
I'm madly in love with a man I've never met
Then as I began to fall,
I'm caught by the quick and smooth hands
of the man at the drums,
beating down and showing out in his territory,
forcing me to imagine myself as his instrument
cause every now and again I like it rough,
every now and again man handle me
till I scream enough is enough,
then at that absolute moment
when I can't take no more of the musical pounding,
he begins to gently tap on the high sounding symbols
till it screams his name,
he's so unpredictable,
he makes the love in my heart come alive and be visible,
going from one sound to the next,
sometimes it feels better than sex,
because regardless the location or who it comes from,
true love is involved,
never failing to evolve into the woman I'm meant to be
The woman who offers the key

to the man on the keys,
as I watch his fingers dance on the black and whites,
my mind starts to drift
and he takes me to higher heights,
all up and down the scale,
creating perfect harmony,
I start to think he's the one for me,
he makes beautiful music
and all I can think about is
how I want to dance,
not giving a damn the style of music he plays
cause as long as his fingers are on that board,
my fingers press record,
never wanting to forget how he makes me feel,
this collaboration is so damn surreal,
someone please explain how can I feel
his fingers start at the top of my left shoulder blade
then walk to the center where my spine is laid,
never failing to keep it moving on pass the small of my back,
feels like he got a handful of my ass and I must say I like that,
pulling me in closer to embrace these lips,
Then all of a sudden I'm pulled away at the hips
by the longwinded man with the wet wood chip
he has perfected the sexaphone,
I mean he has perfected the saxophone,
something about the addition of jazz
that makes me wanna show this musician a better view of ass,
cause what he has to say is whispered so gently into my ear
makes me take long deep breaths until it disappears,
like he's the grim reaper
that takes my ever so last God given breath,
so effortlessly I experience a beautiful death,
I just died in his arms tonight
and it was nothing he said,
better yet it was the fact that I was mislead to believe that
it don't get any better
Then at the second I think it don't get any better,

I am caressed and corrected
by the guitarist that makes majestic love
to his electric squire vintage,
he clutches it like it's the love of his life,
like the very first time a man has kissed his wife,
like he wouldn't know what to do with himself
if it would ever leave his sight,
like in spite of the multitude of viewers
he's taken me like a thief in the night,
like the fact that I am convinced that he is Mr. Right,
then wait...
I'm surprised by the unexpected,
the music drops,
and for that abrupt three seconds
I stand as a woman who longs for the love of her life,
lost and searching for love,
for companionship,
for affection,
confused by the out of body experience
that I'm sure I just experienced
but unable to prove,
because the thing that I love the most
is no longer in my presence,
they have selfishly taken away the reason I live in this moment,
the reason I am even here,
you see I was created to love and be loved
but what I love the most has disappeared,
so now that beautiful death that I have spoken of
has never been more real
but this time it's not as beautiful as before,
I died a horrible death
like being pushed from the 50th floor
of the building that I've called home,
the home that every night I looked forward to lay my dome,
my dome that constantly meditated on the love of my life,
my life that's predestined to make love to music,
Yes music,

he is the only one who can have me at any time,
in any position,
where ever he chooses,
we can have a threesome ,
a ménage a trois',
an orgy
or even become swingers
but the best thing about this rooted love is
the love making we do on the dance floor,
he is my partner and he loves me a whole lot better
than anyone I've ever had before,
never in need of protection
for my heart
cause this connection was safe and secured from the start,
and as he crosses the threshold of my essence,
I exhale
and begin to thank the Omnipresence for
music

Sandy Hook

A moment of silence for the young souls that were ripped from fragile bodies
And the innocent staff that protected scared children in the Sandy Hook School lobby
My heart goes out to all the families that were robbed of precious loved ones
By a heartless self-centered vessel whose weapon was his gun
Today I pray for peace that may seem so far away
For hope for a better tomorrow in spite of this horrific day
I stand speechless and heartbroken witnessing the evils of this world
Not understanding harm done to something worth more than diamonds and pearls
The little children
Whose beautiful heartbeat came to an end in the blink of an eye
The little children
Ending a vulnerable and pure being is the reason why I cry
The little children
Who had wrapped presents at home up under the Christmas tree
The little children
Who's gone too soon to live angelic and heavenly
I can't even imagine the burdens in their mother's heart
Or the weight on their father's shoulders having to deal with time apart
The principal, the teachers and the staff there on duty
Truly they will not be forgotten for their educational beauty
Pray,
And again I say pray
Not only for the victims
But for the whole world in every way
This tragedy on the 14th day in December of O twelve
Let it cause One Love to come forth and to dwell...

A Newborn's Prayer

My first breath of air was paired with my unspoken prayer
Heavenly Father please let him know that I need him,
Walk with him daily and for no reason, leave him
He without you is me without him
Leaving stakes high and chances slim
Let him know the importance of days at the park
I want to hear from him, to be home before dark
Call him to be that man of integrity
Bless him with the privilege of living longevity
Cause there are many events waiting for us to attend
Reasons to show why he is my friend
Encouraging words when I wanna give up
Bedtimes when it's his turn to tuck
He may see me as his bundle of joy
But to me he's so much more
He's that strong hand to protect me
That long hand to reach out for me
That laboring hand to provide for me
That wise hand that will guide me
That righteous hand that disciplines me
That loving hand unconditionally
That is why I hold tight for dear life
Blessed to have his hand
My father
Not another disappointing statistic or
Outlaw, deadbeat, full of reprobate characteristics
My father
Not the one full of broken promises, and missed games
Dodging phone calls because he's so full of shame
My father
Never leaving me to be the duty of a single mother
Or disappearing, forcing me to be raised by another
My father
Selfless, open handed man cradling his baby girl
I am his world within this world

Hoping to find similarities with like qualities of my dad
Knowing what I have in this man
Whose hand I hold
Whose heart is pure as gold
Who can't be bought or sold
My dad
Thank you Heavenly Father for...
my dad

These walls

Writings on the wall that guards the center of my essence
Graffiti of him the artist
Calligraphy of his words that's pressed against the barricade built for my protection
It's like the pain of a tattoo
Just because I can take it doesn't mean it doesn't hurt
A blow to my defenses with every intention to subvert
Or completely destroy the four chambered pump
That supply life to my existence
The vital source of what's left of my cardio system
The root of life, love and purpose
He ask me to come from behind the wall
He wants me vulnerable and naked
Thin skinned and unprotected
But why should I
I see the darts in his hands
Ready to be thrown just to see if I withstand
Testing my endurance
Arresting my assurance
Wanting to surrender but it's safer this way
He supposed to protect me but from what I see it's hard to say
So I stand behind these walls because it's more dependable
It's this very spot that a broken heart is preventable
China built a wall
Protection that made history
The walls of Jericho collapsed
Giving those outside of it victory
I will not be defeated
This wall was built with purpose
Sun up to sun down
Never losing its ground
Keeping me safe and sound
I must say it's my defense mechanism
But it's meant to protect me not you
And there ain't nothing I can do

You gave me reason to see you as the enemy
And until proven otherwise
That is what you'll be to me

Solider of Love

Bleeding
From the fatal blow to my heart
Stretched out on this battle field
Doomed from the start
Crimson stained
Fighting to maintain the little life left in me
As my enemy holds victory
Standing over me
Just to watch how I grasp the exit wound in my chest
Pondering the cold hard metal that entered my back
Caught off guard, none the less
As I was held from behind
Loved with the only sight of it in mind
Thinking there were no need for armory
No need for weapon
No need for fear
But that day I was taught a lesson
Can't have love without war
Love is more precious than diamonds and gold
Rubies and pearls
But it can't be sold
So there must be war to fight for it
Unfortunately
The one you have to fight
Is the one you want to share it with
I wish I'd known before
That wanting it means I would have to die for it
The beat in my heart
I'd be sacrificing it
Building the alter
To lay my heart on the line
Divine destiny
Love wins every time
So with my last breath I call upon 1LoVE

He hears my plea
Rushing to my rescue
To restore life in me

Love you more

The pane of my window drenched in liquid clouds,
Strong thunders roar while I lay here
Needing you
Wanting you
Haunting thoughts of you
Leaving me
Not needing me
But then I'm reminded of 1LoVE
Trusting what I feel within
Not rushing what has not been
I see you
And every authentic fiber of your being
And even what has fail to be seen
One thing I know for sure
And that is that you love me
But I will always love you more…

Power of Seduction

Captured by the passion that overflows
From deep desires buried in her soul
Unaware of her dominance you wave white flag
To an infatuated desire to pack an overnight bag
Prepared to fall victim and candidly pacify
The villain that caught you with one wink of the eye
You easily bit bait so now the hard work is done
From this moment on you are considered her fun
The erotic touch from voluptuous lips
Sends masculine hands down around her hips
You pull her in closer thinking you're in control
But her being your master is the truth untold
Your weakness grew as her attire began to shed
She found that out by the swelling of your head
So eager to know her innermost lining
You deliver yourself as she waits there lying
On the bed her wait was very much brief
You rushed to become one with the commander in chief
Your blood is like supersonic rapid through your veins
Cause your heart is pumping faster to add measure to your brain
Within then without while never exiting her frame
You bare no shame to cry out her name
In the heat of the moment you both gain pleasure
But her pleasure started long before you got together
It started when she noticed you looking suave across the room
She was glad that she was dressed to kill while wearing her best perfume
She patrolled your surroundings feeling certain that you would look
Simultaneously, she was the bait and the hook
She reeled you in and held you tight so that you wouldn't break free
She's a master at what she does, nothing like a trainee

The more time had advance, the more you desired to know her
While the kitty in her pants never concluded to purrrrr
Now you two lay in conjunction of one another
She loudly uttered moans then she said she want it rougher
It turned you on to hear her moan, you felt it coming fast
You pulled it out and made a shift for effective view of ass
The change of position was highly necessary
Every point of view to you was quite contrary
The look in her eye as you lie superior
Coincide with every breath she took as you engaged her interior
With her ass in your hands as she's up on her knees
You guide her back and forward utilizing your squeeze
While time stood still for you she was on the clock
Her job was to lure you in and be your stumbling block
Millions of thoughts run through your head but one is on her mind
That is, the power of seduction works every time

What Do You See?

What do you see when you look upon me
Is it just another girl who needs be delivered from her iniquity?
Maybe you can't see pass this brown covering that signifies diversity
And just cause that, some see one who's full of impurity
You look my way and you see a single mother of four
Then your mind starts to speak to itself and say girl, I know she don't want more
When you witness tears upon my face like it's a facial décor
Do you see trials and tribulations wrestling me to the floor?
Some of you can't help but see the imperfections upon my physique
Doing a serious examination and judgment as if your name is critique
When I suffer defeat and have no words to speak
Is that you on the corner publicizing my losing streak?
When you catch sight of my shady and ungodly ways
Are you confused on Sunday morning when I come up in here and give my God praise?
Do you not know my praise brings cleansing like a menstrual phase?
My praise guarantees me to never become the process of becoming inferior like something that decays
You see, something that decays is nothing but a gradual decrease
And that I know not of, as if I was its long lost niece
You discover my struggle and find it hard to believe that I am full of increase
They say with all that misfortune, how can she ever make peace?
They say, with all of her shortcomings, God loving her makes no sense
They say, the precious blood being shed on her behalf, was a vain expense

You would think the piercing stare from onlookers would cause her to put up a strong defense
But instead, you see her praise, you see her worship, is far more intense
What is it that you hear when you harken unto my voice?
Please don't think I'm just another lady who speaks like this by choice
When you hear my praise, you would think I was just given a brand new Rolls Royce
Truth be told, I have greater reasons to rejoice
You see, I rejoice because He watches me the same way His eye is on that bird
I rejoice because just like Mary I too was impregnated with the Word
I rejoice because when He gave up the ghost He left with us the third
That third being the comforter, the Holy Spirit, in case you haven't heard
Elohim, my God is the reason why my hands shall elevate
It is on His love that He has for me and even has for us that I daily meditate
It is in His holy presence that I desire to marinate and saturate and celebrate and even educate this puny mental state
My life to Him, is what I dedicate
For the moment I was taken in between my matron and sire of mold
Only was I closely acquainted with my dwelling of a monarch and passages of gold
My creator had a purpose for my essence foretold
In this walk of life at this appointed time it was I He enrolled
It was I He enrolled in spite my covering of sin
It was I He invested something greater within
It is for I that He has shut the mouths of the beast in the lion's den
It is my ultimate and absolute destiny to victoriously win
Because I'm stronger than any stone you were ever planning to cast at me

My faith is great enough to divide any hindrance sea
I know that the favor of God is much more valuable than any master's degree
The duty of I, in the body of Christ is that well needed bended knee
Thinking on the woman who struggled with the issue of blood
Her sickness was made public so they drug her name through the mud
Realizing the Messiah was the only to dry up her flood
So she pressed through the crowd like an addict after a drug
with that same determination, I seek my Father's face
In the mist of all my haters, in His presence is my hiding place
Although the world would try to capture you and throw you into a prisoner's base
I can't be caught cause I was given the perfect shoes to run this race.

I can't wait

I can't wait
I can't wait to be held in the arms
Of the two that love me the most
My mother and my father
I can't wait to say adios
To my comfort zone
This womb that's my home before home
My mansion in the sky
That I would gladly say goodbye to
Just to see your faces
Just to feel your kisses upon my cheeks
And your love that's not far reached
I can't wait
I can't wait to take my first breath of air with you
Creating a moment that I'm anxious to share with you
Because I need you
Like hydrogen needing oxygen to be whole like water
I need you
Not just for the days at the park
Or just for your comfort if I am afraid of the dark
But for your love that manifest itself
As a gentle rock to sleep
Or you teaching me that whatsoever I sow, I reap
Wise words
I can't wait
I can't wait to be your bundle of joy
While bundled with joy and love
Because that's what you have for me
And I promise to not give you half of me
Cause you both have all of me
Willingly sharing the privilege
To say that we are family
And as I patiently wait
For my debut
I contemplate
How I will live up to
Your awesomeness
But never doubting that I can
Cause I am
Santana Robert White

Dedication to Baby Santana
Flesh must die

Some people ask
Why would God send His
Only begotten son to
Die for the sins of
You and I
Who's obviously not worthy of
The greatest act of love
Some people ask
How is it that
The man with all power in His hands
Allow other men to
Capture and judge him
Fracture and bruise him
Choose to accuse him
Of wrong doing
When he's done no wrong
Some people ask
If he's the Son of God
Why not get down off that cross
Why not vanish and get lost
So no one can find him
Bind him
Be undermined by mankind
Some people ask
Couldn't he ask
His father to destroy
The task at hand
Deploy an army to stand
For him
Demand his release
From the enemy
Well maybe
Flesh had to die
Be crucified
For you and i
Beaten like the guilty that it is
Weakened by the power that's within
Why do you think
The word says
Flesh must die daily

It wasn't talking about
Pushing up daisies
But killing the power of sin
And allow your spirit man to begin
To take its rightful place
Flesh must die
However you wanna do it
Starve it
Deprive it
Drive it over a cliff
And don't revive it
Because it wants to control you
Choke hold your soul
Giving you the only life it has to offer
And that's a life's sentence without bail
In the fiery pits of hell
The only way to truly live
Is to die to self
Now before misunderstanding
Creeps in
And inhabit your mind
Of what I'm saying
I'm not talking about
Putting an end to your life
But just say no to the desires of your flesh
It is of this world
It doesn't want to love
It wants lust
Infatuation
Damnation fornication
It doesn't want truth
It wants fabricated lies
Perfect place to hide
What needs be seen
And all that's in between the absolute truth
Don't want righteousness
Or holiness
Just our sins thrown into the sea of forgetfulness
Using the fact that we all fall short
As an excuse to fall short
Using the fact that we all fall short
As an excuse to fall short
Using the fact that we all fall short

As an excuse to fall short
Consult the power invested into your spirit
There's a battle between it and dust
Between love and lust
Between just and all that's unjust
The only way your spirit wins
Is to kill the flesh
But now a day your flesh wins
Because it stands stronger
We feed and cater to its hunger
Starving the essence of your soul
Rejecting the blessings to be whole
Spiritually
In his image we were made first
But some how
Roles have been reversed
Making self a priority
While simultaneously
Spirit sits on the back burner
Dying of starvation
Pleading for conversation
With our father
Needing fruits of the spirit
While flesh treats it like
The homeless man on the corner
Begging for bread
Turning a blind eye and deaf ear
To opportunity for charity
More concerned with our image
Than the image of God
Blaming Satan
For our mishaps
When nine times out of ten
He comes as temptation
Thinking that
Perhaps
We'd give in
So
Open your eyes to see
The crucifixion for what it is
Killing of flesh
Lashing
And piercing

Binding
And controlling
Placing under subjection
Everything that's not like God
Being in this world but not of this world
Living in the spirit
Giving all that's needed to be victorious over the flesh
It is impossible for the individualist called self to be perfect
But God said be ye perfect
For I am perfect
But He is spirit
So tap into the power of your spirit man
That's where you can stand as perfection

My Heart in Your Hand

My heart knows

Every detail of your hand

Blood drip from the tip of my apex

Streaming like a river

Through your heart line

That defines

The amount of time

On this side of heaven

That belongs to us

My heartbeat

And your pulse

Synced

Union together

Like our ancestors

Who would never part ways

Even on bad days and nights

Toughing it out

Knowing its gon be alright

My heart knows

Every detail of your hand

The exact angles

In the joints

As it declares my love

Repairs my love

And never compare my love

To its past love

Safe and secured

Like a baby in its mom's arms

Protecting it from hurt, harm or danger

Not questioning

If your hand

Can hold my heart

For ever

Cause without a shadow of doubt

I know that it can

Withstand the test of times

And for whatever reason

It might stop beating

Your hand

Will force feed

My heart beat of life

Even if it shortens your life line

That runs from thumb side

To the base of your palm

You keep calm

Knowing it won't be long

Before our love is revived

Meant for each other

Like a hand in glove

Kept warm with love of a soul mate

Never overweight

Cause you're strong enough

To take on the baggage I may have

Some extra fatty tissue that's affixed

To the walls of my heart

Not knowing that the fire

That burns within

Burns to shed pounds of the unwanted weight

At a rapid rate

My heart knows

Every detail of your hand

Length and width

Precisely calculated

Knowing the exact location of jaded scars

From love and war

Grooves and indentations

That's the perfect place to get comfortable in

I rest

In diastole

Embodying maximum capacity

From left to right

Top to bottom

In the palm of your hand

I rest

In diastole

Having the audacity

To boldly take ownership

Of this hand and heart relationship

I rest

In the palm of your hand

Weighs me down

It weighs me down

I can't take another step with it on my back

So I act fast before it kills me

Too much for me to bare

So I go to God in prayer

Because maybe

He doesn't see me

Struggling to continue

Never wanting to give up

But listen

I can't take another step

Not forward

Not even backwards

So I drop to my knees

And put my head to the ground

Downward spiral is the direction I move in now

I wanna elevate my hands

Total surrender you know

But these unclean hands

Are my dirtiest member

So I dip them in

The nearest holy water

And that's my pool of tears

Because it is pure

With righteous purpose

Not really sure if it will work

But it's my last option

Before I give in

To this load

Before I forfeit

Hopes of being whole again

One Love

Brace yourselves black people

God is not a black man

He's not covered in skin of color

He's not your brother from another mother

He didn't derive from Africa

Where skin needed to be darker

He doesn't have hair

That's kinky or nappy

Cornrowed or dreaded

Damn right I said it

He's larger than that

Race is what divides us

Covers up what's inside of us

Similarities

That prove we are one of the same

But you're too busy trying to proclaim

That God is a black man

Why?

Do you not know that

Race is of this world

It is flesh from the dust of the grounds

That surrounds what makes us equal

Given to us as a people

To contain the feel of liveliness

The amount of pigments in your skin

Is only the superficial

God runs deeper than skin deep

And the skin we're in is the weakest of the weak

Flesh

Regardless of its color

Makes us unlike angels

His image is spirit

And spirit only

He is the universe and beyond

He's love that burst to be shared

Burst through anything that tries to contain him

He knows no color

He is light

And I don't mean he's white or Caucasian

Fail not to get lost in translation

He's not the blond haired

Blue eyed man in the pictures

He's not the black words

Or the white pages

Of the scripture bible

Or the Quran

Nor to rah

He is God

The great I am

He's not in the box

So stop trying to put him there

He exceeds past the universe

He's a multiverse

Full of diversity

Mysteriously existing

With no boundaries or limitations

He is the absolute creator of all creations

Alpha and Omega

He has no common descent

Especially no heredity

And although I can't explain

The fullness of his existence

I know that he's not a black man

Neither white, Asian or Hispanic

And there's no need to panic

Thinking that you can't relate

To a God that's not like you

Cause you were created in his image

Clothed in agape

So put away your reasons

To divide up one race

The human race

Unity is stronger

Than a segmented nation

Practice one love

Marry the idea of wholeness

And know that it will take boldness

To go against a system

That fails to work but rules supreme

A system that segregate us as human beings

Brothers and sisters

We are different

This is true

I don't know about you

But there's more to me than what meets the eye

Not defined by the color of my skin

Texture of my hair

Or the hood that I live in

One God

One race

One love

It's yours

Hey

I'm just gonna jump to the chase

And say

I'm late

I haven't gotten my cycle

That cleanses me

I guess I'm filthy

And expecting

And it's yours

You did this to me

How could I let it be?

I wanna abort it

Or miscarry

But I'm scared

What the fuck you mean

How's it yours

You entered inside me

Broke walls that I had up for guard

Now I'm carrying something

Not of God

Bastard child

Oh my God !

I feel it growing rapidly

Feeding off of me

I just want it out of me

I don't need to name it

Cause it has a name

More than one

But they're all the same

Doubt fear trust issues

Too late to choose the right thing to do

Now I'm damaged goods

At the baggage claim

But you failed to claim

What's rightfully yours

Not man enough

To stand and face the truth

It's yours

This burden you help create

I don't want it no more

It's an evil seed

You planted in me

It intends to take control

Mishandling me

No OB/GYN

Cause I'm not with child

The look upon your face is priceless

A beguiled stare

Filled with wonder

Of what life is growing

In the womb of my existence

A persistent creature

Who wants to claim me?

My life and all that I have

So if I have to go through

This misery we created

So do you

It's only fair

To admit the truth…………..It's yours

Lily in the Valley

Disturbing darkness

Overpowers the mist of the valley

Low dry place

That feed off unfamiliar faces

That comes and goes

Just to pass through

Traveling souls

Finding it hard to ignore the view

Of decomposed flesh

Of a dying age

Decayed nature

That is lifeless

Prolonged crisis

That cries from grounds

Stained of death

The valley

That reaps sorrows

That it hasn't sown

But somehow

Beauty has grown

Right in the eye of it

Stand out like a sore thumb

Difficult to miss

But makes you wonder

How?

How did the lily in the valley

Come to exist

Were good seeds planted

By vile hands

Or were virtuous hearts

Inhabiting the land

That has come to be what it is

Or is it just impossible

For something to be

Without its opposite

The valley and the lily

Diametric relationship

That co-exist

To appear strange

But never the less

Beautiful in the eye that rest upon it

There's a lily in the valley

And it has been found to be bright

As the morning star

Defeating the shadows

Of opposition

Outshining the work of gallows

While bodies still hang in the balance

Of an unbalanced territory

Crowned in glory

Petals of purity

Aromas scent of majesty

I mean it makes no sense

Of crashing tragedies

That is thrown together

And actually works artistically

Is the same life

That gives life to a dying soil

The source of life

For alabaster box

Filled with fragrant oils

Or does the precious flower

Absorb the life out of the valley

Just too selfishly stand alone

And thrive

One will never know

Unless you are that lily

Or that valley

To give voice to its madness

To answer question

And explain wonders

Of opposing attractions

Married together

As perfection

www.ingramcontent.com/pod-product-compliance
Lightning Source LLC
Chambersburg PA
CBHW020658300426
44112CB00007B/438